Electricity

Contents

Revision

Did you know . . . ?

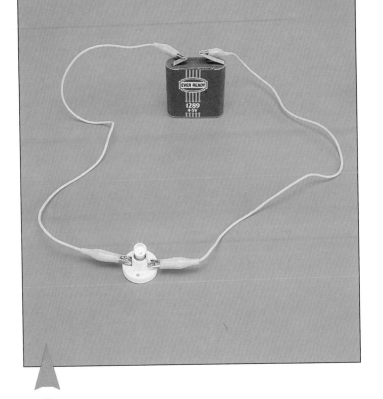

⭐ **A complete circuit is needed for an electric current to flow.**

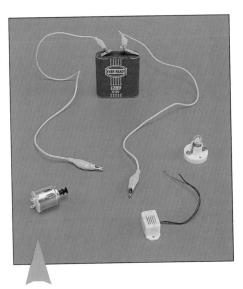

⭐ **We can use different components in a circuit to do different jobs.**

⭐ **A switch can be used to stop an electric current from flowing. Materials which are conductors allow electricity to flow.**

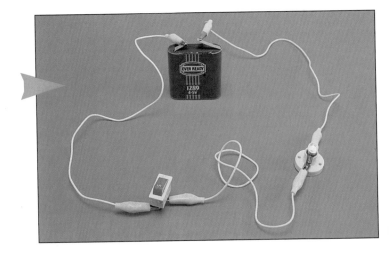

For electricity to flow it needs a complete circuit.

Electricity flows from both ends of the battery to the bulb.

If you cut a wire, all the electricity runs out into the room.

Electricity is always safe.

Flat batteries are empty.

Electricity only goes through the bulb. It uses up all the electricity.

Electricity flows one way, from one terminal on a battery to the bulb and then to the other terminal on the battery.

Task 1

Think about electricity

* These children shared their ideas about electricity and batteries.

* Which ideas do you agree with? Why?

* Which ideas don't you agree with? Why?

PCM 1

* Make two lists.
  Use Photocopy Master 1.

* Now make a booklet for young children to show how to use electricity safely.

I agree with this idea	I disagree with this idea
	'Electricity is always safe' because . . .

Make a bulb light up in a circuit

- Design and make a name card for your desk.

- Use a circuit to make part of your name light up.

◆ Now try this

- Put a motor in the circuit to make part of your name spin around.

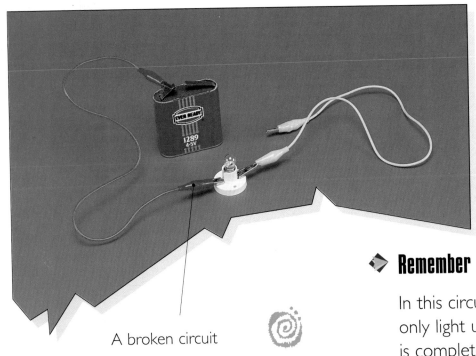

A broken circuit

◆ Remember

In this circuit the bulb will only light up if the circuit is complete.

Electricity can only flow around the circuit if the circuit has no gaps.

If the circuit is broken, the electricity cannot flow and the bulb will not light.

Different types of battery

There are many different types of batteries.
In this book you will see 4.5 V batteries. If you do not have a 4.5 V battery, you could use three 1.5 V batteries.

How much energy the battery has depends on what type it is.

The amount of energy in a battery is measured as **volts (V)** or **voltage**.
The number on the battery shows you the voltage.

 Make a collection of batteries.

 Read the voltage on each battery.

 Record what you find out.

This is a 1.5 V battery.
One cylinder like this is called a cell.
Some batteries are made up of two or more cells.

This is a 4.5 V battery.
1.5 V + 1.5 V + 1.5 V = 4.5 V

Task 4 — Conductors and insulators

- Do you remember what a **conductor** is? Make a list of eight things that conduct electricity.

- Do you remember what an **insulator** is? Make a list of eight things that are insulators.

Task 5 — Conductor tester

- Make a 'conductor tester' - a model that can test whether different things are conductors.

- Make a set of instructions to explain how the conductor tester works.

- Try out your conductor tester on the things you listed for Task 4.

- Use Photocopy Master 2 to show your results.

Do It Yourself switch

- Remember – you can make a switch to put in a circuit to turn things on and off.

- Make a DIY leaflet which tells someone else how to make a switch for a circuit.

- Use pictures, diagrams and words.

- Give your leaflet to a friend to use.

  You might use a computer to word-process your leaflet.

PCM 3

- Now make your switch and check that it works.
  Use Photocopy Master 3 to show how you made your switch.

Electricity consumer

We all use electricity every day, probably without thinking about it.

Katrina kept an 'Electricity Diary' for a day. She made a note of every time she used electricity.

✦ Keep your own electricity diary for one day, just like Katrina did.

✦ When you have kept your diary for a day, work out
- how many different **electrical appliances** you used
- how many minutes of electricity you need each day.

Electrical appliances are all things that need electricity to make them work.

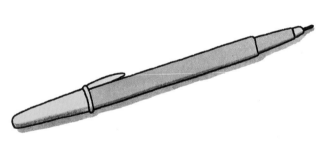

⚠ Safety point: Be very careful with all things that use electricity.

Katrina's Diary

Tuesday

7.15 am	Radio alarm woke me up.
7.20 am	Switched bedside lamp on.
7.21 am	Turned radio off.
7.24 am	Switched bathroom light on.
7.26 am	Had a shower – electric.
7.40 am	Back in bedroom – dried hair with hairdryer.
7.55 am	Downstairs for breakfast. Put kettle on. Put radio on. Put toaster on. Put light on.

◆ Think about

- How you could carry out a survey to find out how many different electrical appliances children in your class used?
- How you could find out who uses the most electricity in your class?

Use a computer to record your surveys.

Paying for electricity

 Read this electricity bill.

 How many units of electricity were used?

 How much does a unit of electricity cost?

 How much of the total cost was not for units of electricity?

◆ Now try this

 Bring an electricity bill from home.

 Read your electricity bill.

 How many units did your household use?

 How much does your electricity cost per unit?

Middle Electric Ltd S Brown 8 High Street South Field	Your account No. 013 2148 6322 Date of account 19 October Tariff - D1 Domestic
	AMOUNT
£ p	£ p
Quarterly charge 22 08	22 08
(Unit charges 7 20)	
Current reading 18/10 178 96	
Previous reading 05/05 161 01	
Units used 17 95	
1795 units @ 7.20p	129 24
Total charge	151 32

Save it

 Find out what kind of things use electricity around the school.

 Record what you find out.

 How much is the school electricity bill? Find out.

 How could your school reduce its electricity bill?

 Think of some different ways that you could save electricity around the school.

 Make an Action Plan for your school to help save electricity.

Things that use electricity	Number of these things around the school
Lights	87
Computers	5
School alarm	1

⭐ **Circuit diagrams are special ways of showing a circuit.**

Fact File

Electrical symbols

There are special symbols for drawing diagrams of electric circuits.

Switches are usually drawn like this.

Wires must always be drawn as a straight line, using a ruler, except when wires cross.

wires crossing

connecting wire

two wires joined

Batteries are made up of cells.

one cell

two cells

three cells

These are the symbols for the different components used in circuits. The bulb is also known as a lamp.

motor

bulb (lamp)

buzzer

bell

When you draw a circuit diagram it is important to use a ruler and draw straight lines. A circuit diagram is always drawn as a box.

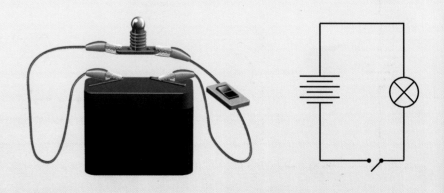

Task 10 Drawing circuits

Here are some pictures of circuits.

Draw the circuit diagram for each picture. Use the symbols on page 10.

①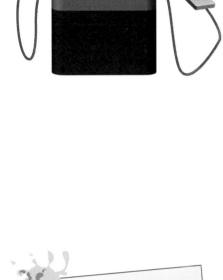

②

③

you need:
- wire
- battery
- bulbs
- switches
- electric buzzer
- motor

Task 11 Making circuits

Here are some circuit diagrams. Make each one of the circuit diagrams. Show your teacher your circuits.

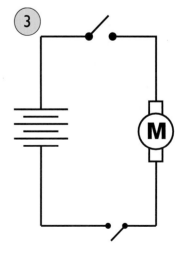

①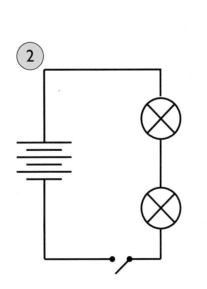

②

③

Fabulous pictures

Sanjay created this fabulous
picture. The monster's eyes
light up in the picture.
He also drew a diagram
of the circuit in his picture.

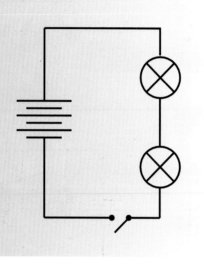

Design and make your own fabulous
picture.
Show your design on Photocopy
Master 4.

It should use a circuit to make
something light up, move or make
a noise.
Which component or components will
you use in your picture?

When you have finished, draw a diagram
of your circuit.

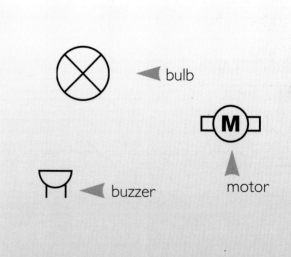

bulb

motor

buzzer

electric bell

Which diagram?

Match each sentence to the correct circuit diagram.

 PCM 5

Write down your answers on Photocopy Master 5.

① Bell working without a switch.
② Bulb working without a switch.
③ Motor working with a switch.
④ Buzzer working with a switch.
⑤ Bell working with a switch.
⑥ Two bulbs working with a switch.

 PCM 6

Draw circuit diagrams to match the models in the pictures on Photocopy Master 6.

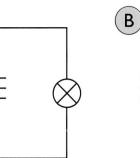

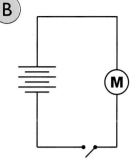

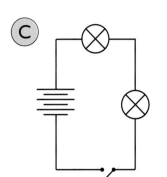

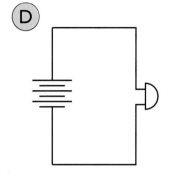

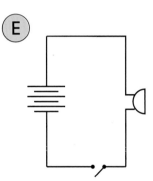

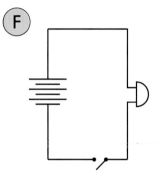

Snap and pairs

Make a set of circuit cards which you can use to play snap or pairs with a friend.

First make a set of cards of circuit pictures.

Then make matching cards of circuit diagrams.

Have a game of Snap.

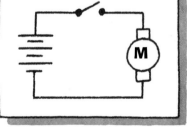

Batteries then and now

The first battery was made in 1794 by an Italian scientist called Alessandro Volta.

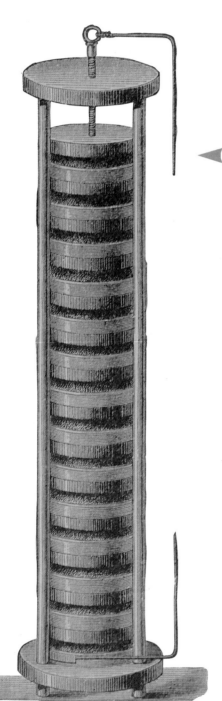

The first battery did not look like the batteries we use today. Volta's battery looked like a tower of sandwiches. It was made from cardboard soaked in acid which was placed between discs of copper and zinc.
A special change that happens between the zinc, copper and cardboard dipped in acid makes electricity.

Today, batteries come in all shapes and sizes. They are more powerful than Volta's first battery. They are also much easier to carry around and use!

Benjamin Franklin
1706-1790

Sir Humphry Davy
1778 -1829

Thomas Edison
1847-1931

Michael Faraday *1791-1867*

Task
15
Famous discoverers

✪ Research information about some people who have made discoveries to do with electricity.
Use Photocopy Master 7 to show what you find out.

Task
16
Make a simple battery

✪ Try making this simple battery.

✪ For this task you will use a Light Emitting Diode (LED). LEDs do not need a lot of electricity to light up. LEDs only work if they are connected the right way round - when the longer leg is connected to the positive side of the battery.

The pieces of zinc and copper must all be the same size, about $5\frac{1}{2}$ cm long and $1\frac{1}{2}$ cm wide.

⚠ Use a kitchen knife to make a slit in the lemons for the pieces of zinc and copper. Do not try to push them in.

you need:
- piece of zinc
- piece of copper
- wires with crocodile clips
- LED
- 2 lemons

copper   zinc

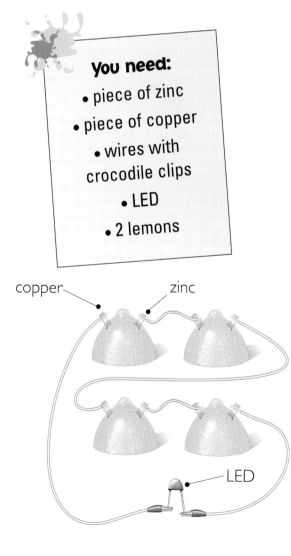

LED

Which battery?

- The *Which?* magazine carried out tests on different Walkman batteries.

- Use the results to answer these questions.

  - Which batteries cost the least per hour to run?

  - Which battery cost the most per hour to run?

  - Equipment which uses a lot of electricity is called **high-drain**. Equipment that does not is called **medium-drain**. Why do you think the batteries in the high-drain equipment, such as a personal stereo, cost more per hour than in the medium-drain equipment, such as a clock?

  - Which battery was best in high - and medium-drain equipment?

  - If you could afford any battery which one would you buy for your personal stereo?

◆ Now try this

- Photocopy Master 8 shows the results of an investigation.
  Draw a bar chart to show the results.

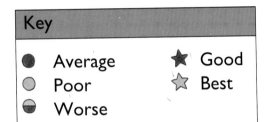

Key			
● Average		★ Good	
○ Poor		☆ Best	
◑ Worse			

AA batteries - information	Company A Long Life	Company B Extra Long Life	Company C Long Life	Company D Energizer	Company E Extra Life	Company F Alkaline	Company G Long Life	Company H Long Life
Price per pack of 4 in £s	2.29	2.99	3.49	3.39	2.99	2.59	2.45	2.45
Country of origin	UK	UK	Belgium	France	USA	Germany	UK	UK
Which Test Results								
Battery Life - medium-drain equipment	○	○	☆	○	○	○	◑	●
Battery Life - high-drain equipment	★	☆	☆	☆	●	☆	☆	☆
Cost per hour in pence - medium-drain equipment	4	5	5	5	6	5	4	4
Cost per hour in pence - high-drain equipment	11	14	16	17	20	14	12	12

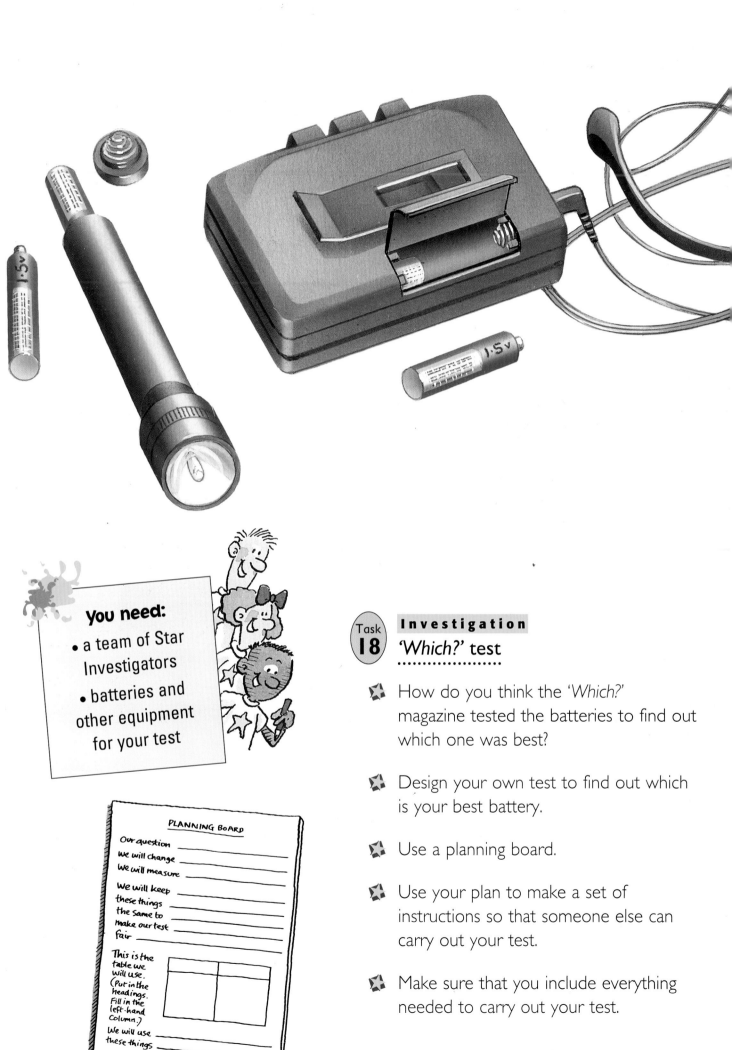

PLANNING BoARD

Our question _____

We will change _____

We will measure _____

We will keep these things the same to make our test fair _____

This is the table we will use. (Put in the headings. Fill in the left-hand column.)

We will use these things _____

Task 18

Investigation

'Which?' test

◆ How do you think the 'Which?' magazine tested the batteries to find out which one was best?

◆ Design your own test to find out which is your best battery.

◆ Use a planning board.

◆ Use your plan to make a set of instructions so that someone else can carry out your test.

◆ Make sure that you include everything needed to carry out your test.

★ We can vary the current in a circuit.

Resistors

Remember – materials that electricity can pass through are called **conductors**. Materials that electricity cannot pass through are called **insulators**.

Electricity does not pass through some materials very easily. Very thin wire and the 'lead' in your pencil (graphite) are two examples. These are called **resistors**.

The wire inside lamps is very thin. Electricity cannot pass through easily. The wire is a resistor.

You can increase the resistance of a material by making it very thin or very long. The longer the wire the greater its resistance.

Task 19   Dimmer and brighter

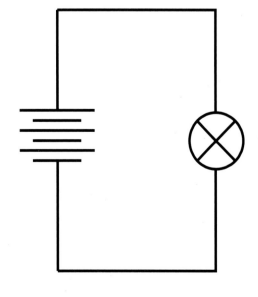

- ✦ Make this circuit.

- ✦ Think of two things you could do which would make the bulb shine dimmer or brighter.

- ✦ Try out your ideas.

- ✦ Draw the circuits you made. Next to each circuit describe what happened.

Task 20

Using a resistor

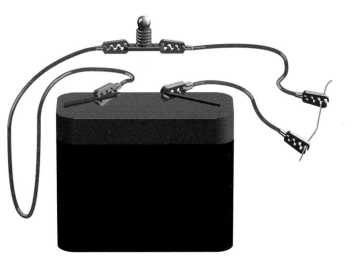

- Make the circuit in the picture.

- Put the thin wire between the crocodile clips as shown in the picture.

- Move one of the crocodile clips along the wire.

- What happens?

- What do you have to do to make the bulb dimmer and brighter?

- Record your results.

PCM 9

- Now try the activity on Photocopy Master 9.

Task 21

Trying a different resistor

You may have already used a pencil 'lead' to make a dimmer switch. (See **Star Science, Lower Junior Pupils' Book**)

You made the dimmer switch using a resistor. The pencil lead is a resistor.

- Make the circuit in the picture.

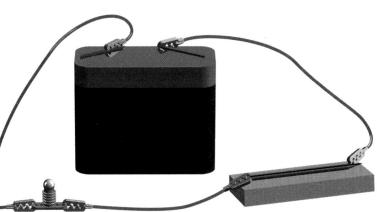

- Slide the crocodile clips backwards and forwards on the pencil lead. Soft lead is best for this.

- What happens?

- What do you have to do to make the bulb dimmer?

- What do you have to do to make the bulb brighter?

The Morse Code

In 1840, an American called Samuel Morse invented a special code. The code used long and short electrical signals. These were sent down telegraph wires.

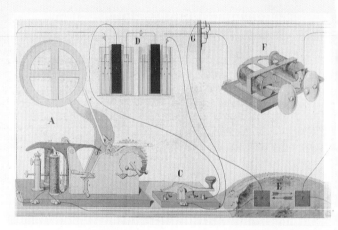

Morse Code transmitter, 1882.

This special type of communication is called Morse Code. The code is written down as dots and dashes. People sending the code press down a special key. The key is held down for a short amount of time for a dot and twice as long for a dash.

A ·−	B −···	C −·−·	D −··
E ·	F ··−·	G −−·	H ····
I ··	J ·−−−	K −·−	L ·−··
M −−	N −·	O −−−	P ·−−·
Q −−·−	R ·−·	S ···	T −
U ··−	V ···−	W ·−−	X −··−
Y −·−−	Z −−··	? ··−−··	FULL STOP ·−·−·−

A Morse Code transmitter

✦ Look at this picture.

✦ Use the materials to make your own Morse Code transmitter.

you need:

- a battery
- a bulb in a bulb-holder
- wires with crocodile clips
- plastic bottle top
- thick card or balsa wood
- copper strip bent into shape
- small screwdriver

Glue the bottle top on. When you press it down, the circuit is complete and the bulb will light up.

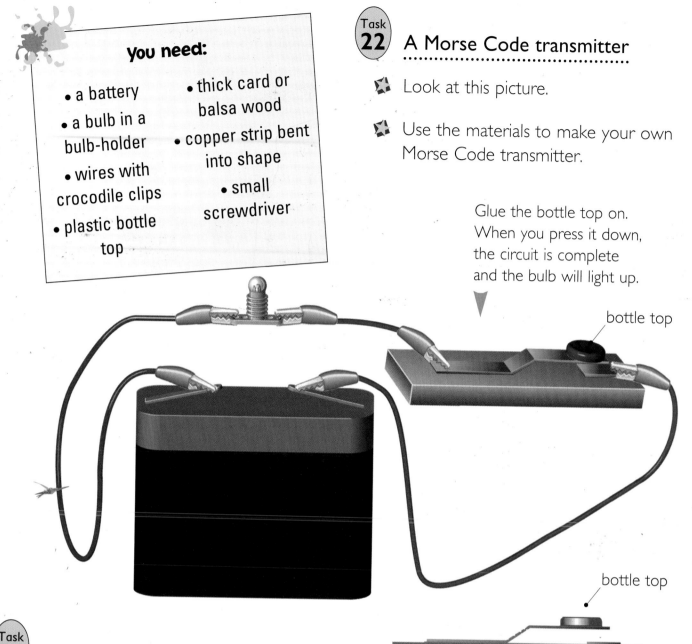

bottle top

bottle top

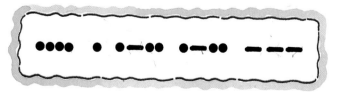

Your name in code

✦ Look at the table on page 20.

✦ Work out your name in Morse Code.

✦ Send your name to your friends. Ask your friend if the message was correct.

✦ Take it in turns with a friend to send a one-word message in Morse Code.

✦ Take it in turns with a friend to send a sentence in Morse Code.
SOS stands for Save Our Souls. It is the signal for people in distress, to ask for help to be sent urgently.

✦ What would the Morse code for SOS be?

✦ Write it down.

✦ What does this Morse Code message say?

Remember it is how long you hold the switch down, not how hard, that sends a dot or a dash signal.

⭐ **Series and parallel are two types of circuit.**

Round and round in circuits

For an electrical current to flow in a circuit, all parts of the circuit must be joined together. The wires, battery, bulbs, motors and other components must all be joined to each other.

There are two different types of electric circuit. One is a **series** circuit. The other is a **parallel** circuit.

you need:
- paper
- stiff card
- coloured pencils
- scissors
- battery
- wire
- bulb-holders
- bulbs
- small screwdriver

(Task 24) **Using a series circuit**

✴ Make a clown's face. Stick it onto stiff card. Cut holes for the eyes and nose.

✴ Make the clown's nose light up.

✴ Make the clown's nose and one eye light up.

✴ Make the clown's nose and both eyes light up.

Task 25

Altering the circuit

When you made the clown's eyes and nose light up using this series circuit, you probably found that either the lamps were very dim or that they did not work.

✦ What do you think would happen if you added a motor to this circuit to spin the pom-pom on the clown's hat?
Try it.

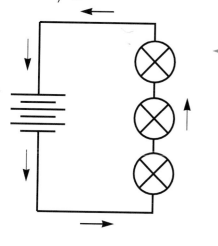

◀ This is a series circuit. In a series circuit, the current flows in one direction.

If one component is taken out it breaks the circuit and all of the other components do not work.

✦ What happens when you add more lamps to the circuit?

✦ What happens if you take a lamp out when the circuit is connected?

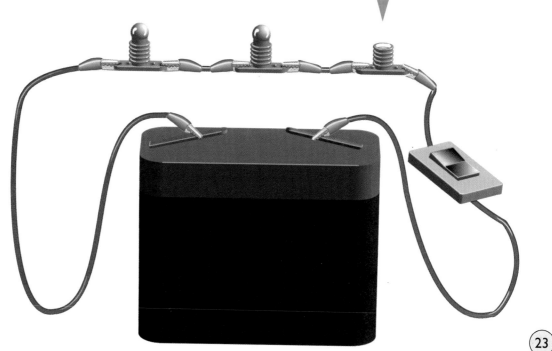

Using a parallel circuit

① In a **series circuit**, the current flows in one direction through all the components. If one component is taken out, then it breaks the circuit and all of the other components do not work.

▼

If this bulb was removed, the circuit would be broken.

▼

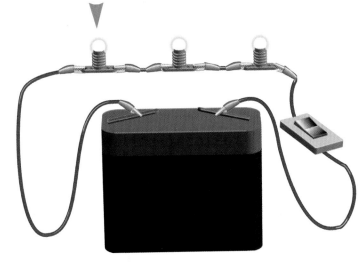

When you made the clown's face in a series circuit, the bulbs were connected in a circle.

② You could also connect the components like this to light up the clown's face.

This is called a **parallel circuit**.
Notice how the wires are drawn parallel to each other.

▼

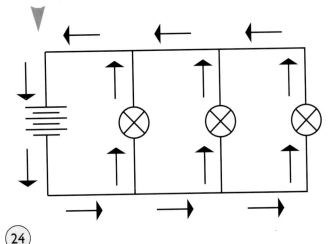

③ In a parallel circuit each component has a circuit of its own.

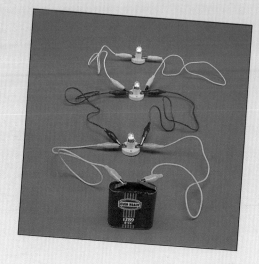

If you took a bulb out, it would not affect the others.

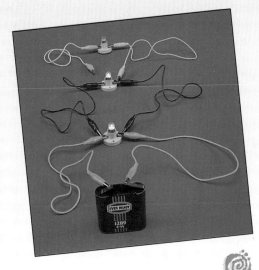

◆ Now try this

✦ Use Photocopy Master 10. Match the circuit diagrams to the correct pictures.

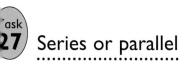

Series or parallel

❋ Make each of these sets of circuits.

❋ Write down observations about each circuit in a table like this.

Use Photocopy Master 11.

Circuit	Observations/Comments	
	Series	Parallel
1		
2		
3		

 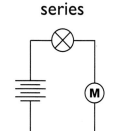 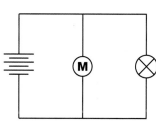

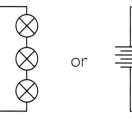 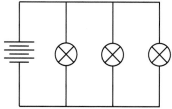

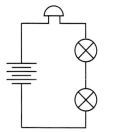 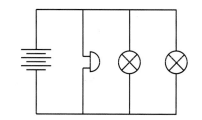

Check your lights!

❋ Make a model of a vehicle.
It could be:

- a car
- a fire engine
- a police car
- an ambulance
- a rescue truck.

❋ You will need some lights.

❋ How will you make sure that the lights work?

❋ What kind of circuit will you use?

❋ Will you use more than one circuit?

Fact File

A special switch

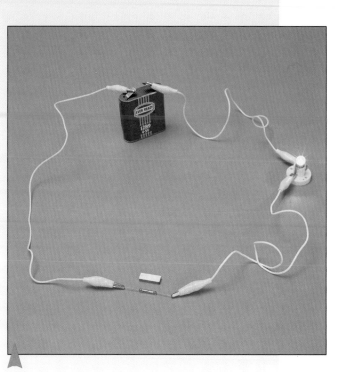

Reed switches need a small magnet to work.

When the magnet is placed near the reed switch, the metal strips close. The circuit is complete and the light is switched on.

When the magnet is moved away from the reed switch, the metal strips separate. The circuit is broken, the switch is off and the light is off.

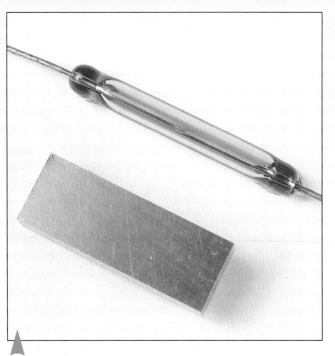

This is a special kind of switch called a reed switch.

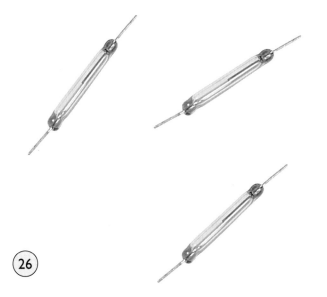

Task 29 Make a model using a reed switch

Use a reed switch in a model to make something switch on and off.

✪ Design, make and try out your own model.

✪ Show it to people in your class.

A tilt switch. Inside the switch there is a ball bearing made of steel. When the tube is tilted, the ball bearing moves to complete the circuit.

This model uses another special switch called a tilt switch. When the handle is moved backwards and forwards, the clown's nose lights up.

✹ Make your own model using a tilt switch.

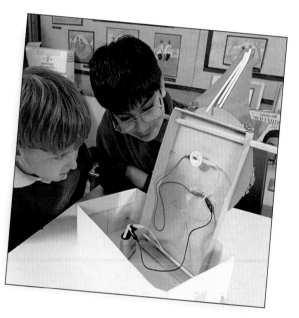

PCM
12

✹ Draw your design on Photocopy Master 12.

✹ Explain how the tilt switch works.

Task 31 Fun at the fair

you need:
- battery
- switch
- small screwdriver
- motor
- bulbs in bulb-holders
- wire
- balsa wood
- dowelling
- cardboard
- glue
- paint
- sellotape

✦ Make a fantastic flying plane ride that works.

✦ Use a motor.

✦ How will you make sure that it is a smooth ride?

✦ How will you make sure that the rides do not fly off?

✦ What kind of circuit will you use?

✦ How will you hide the motor and battery? (Keep how it works a secret!)

✦ Use a parallel circuit to add lights.

PCM
13

✦ Draw your design on Photocopy Master 13.

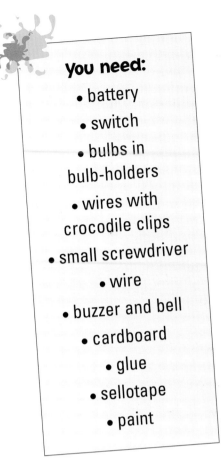

you need:

- battery
- switch
- bulbs in bulb-holders
- wires with crocodile clips
- small screwdriver
- wire
- buzzer and bell
- cardboard
- glue
- sellotape
- paint

Task 32 A haunted room

⚡ Think about things you would find in a haunted room.

⚡ Make a model.

⚡ How will you create different effects with lights?
Can you dim the lights?

⚡ How will you make things move?

⚡ What could you use to make a sound?

⚡ Does part of the circuit needs a series circuit? Why?
Does part of the circuit needs a parallel circuit? Why?

Here is a model of a haunted room.
The ghost spins around and the light flickers.

PCM
14

A. Smile
Production Manager
Happy Toys PLC
Toysville
TS1 1HT

Dear Class

Happy Toys PLC would like to employ you to make a game or a model for young children. The model should use electrical circuits.

It could be a

- toy car with lights
- a quiz game.

When you have designed and made your game or model Happy Toys PLC would like you to send them the following:

- a model of the game or model you make
- a circuit diagram to show how it works
- a set of word-processed instructions on how to make the game or use the model
- a design for the packaging of the game.

You may work individually or with a friend to complete this project.

Yours sincerely

A. Smile

A.Smile (Production Manager)

Electrical Equipment

Here are pictures of some of the basic electrical equipment that you need to carry out the tasks in this book.

batteries and battery holder

bulbs and bulb-holders

LEDs

motor

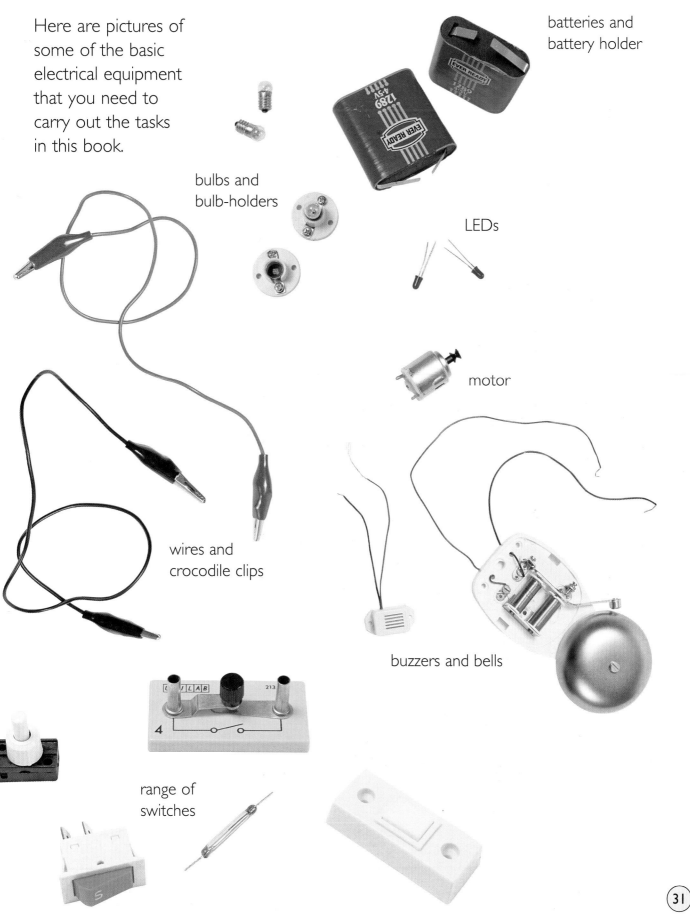

wires and crocodile clips

buzzers and bells

range of switches

Checkpoint

Double check quiz

PCM 15

Show your answers on Photocopy Master 15.

Question 1
What do each of these symbols stand for?

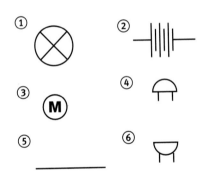

Question 2
Each of the following circuits will work. True or false?

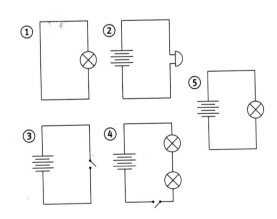

Question 3
Which of the following will conduct electricity from a battery?

- a plastic comb
- a wooden ruler
- pencil lead
- aluminium foil
- tin can
- silver ring

Question 4
Write down three different ways to make a bulb shine dimmer or brighter.

Question 5
Who made the first battery in 1794?

Question 6
Which circuits are parallel circuits?
Which circuit is a series circuit?

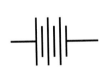

Question 7
What would you do to a circuit with one buzzer to make it sound like a police siren (a 'nee-naw' sound)?

Question 8

How many cells are there in this battery? How many volts do they add up to?

◆ Now try this

PCM 16

Use Photocopy Master 16 to make up your own electricity wordsearch.